Wither and Bloom copyright © by Dominik Shields 2021.
All rights reserved.
No part of this book may be used or reproduced, transmitted in any form electronic, mechanical, recording or otherwise in any manner whatsoever without the authors permission, except in the case of reprints in the case of reviews.
For permissions contact: creativeinktuition@gmail.com

Dominik Shields asserts the moral right to be identified as the author of this work.

Paperback edition 2021
Cover design: Dominik Shields
Edited with love by: Ren Alessandra
Internal formatting: Kaitlyn Hickey
ISBN: 978-0-646-84262-2

EBook edition 2021
ISBN: 978-0-646-84299-8

Published by Creative Inktuition
www.creativeinktuition.com

WITHER & BLOOM

Dominik Shields

This was written for everyone who has had their heartbroken but learned to stitch it back together again on their own

&

for the boy who made it feel like summer time, every single day.

WITHER

I am a hurricane.

Thriving off chaos, destroying the calm of those around me.
The destruction I leave, larger than the love left, swaying in the wind, hoping for a miracle.

There is never a calm before my storm, I am the raging sea
and you,
a mere life raft.

My water never still, my waves never quiet, emotions as turbulent as the howling winds in your ears.

It's as if they never stood a chance.

You created a home.
A cabin tucked in the depths of the woods, a welcomed stillness.
Then I took a match and burnt it to the ground.
I saw myself through the flames as they scorched the safety we created.
I watched as I lit up the illusion of what could have been.

~ no more storybooks.

Do you remember the trip we took?
The one to the place by the lake?
When I couldn't breathe, you held my hand as I sobbed in the shower, searching for breath.

The night air cascading down into my lungs, the dust not settling.
There you were, by my side, with a cup of tea and that look in your eyes.

Where are you now?

Once again, I'm gasping for air on my own.

The boy with lagoon eyes &
the girls heart, raging like the sea,
You would think they fall together in gentle harmony.
Water welcoming water, serenity surrounding them.

Yet the water was too heavy for them to hold, they did not
have the strength to keep fighting.
The love that held them together washed away the day their
barriers broke.

Leaving nothing but puddles of them behind.

As your waves crashed into me, I drank you down.

Filled up every part of my being until your water turned to salt.

I inhale the ghost of you, exhale the memories that keep me awake at night.

I'm not able to let you go, no matter how hard my lungs try.

~ meditative breathing

I bought a devil's ivy to replace you, it withered away the more time I spent with him.

~ this has to be a sign.

The rain reminds me of you, still.

How we would lie curled in fresh sheets, our faces close, sharing silly stories.

How you would cradle my face like it was the most precious thing you would ever hold.

The way your eyes would look into mine
like they never wanted to bathe in another reflection.

A constant ticking in my brain,
a clock that never ends,
time passing but never going anywhere.

Over and over, day in day out, constant humming, constant noise.
I miss when there was silence,
when there was someone filling up my spaces.

If only we had more time.

(Un)fortunately I'm going to love you for the rest of my life.

I thought we would spend forever surrounded by music, our cats and a green velvet sofa.

~ wishes don't come true

Princess, you'd always call me.
Not because of money or attitude, but because you put me so high on a pedestal.

I stay out of reach and untouchable, withering away in my ivory tower, waiting for you to slay the beast in your mind and return to me.

But you never did.

The dragon devoured you, I was left helpless.

As I stayed on my own I became tough, resilient, the soft skin that kept my heart safe and turned cold and callous.
It hardened like scales upon my back.
I spat venom from my mouth to all those that would try to enter.

Time fell away as I did from what we used to be.

I realised was the dragon all along.

Driving you away from me.

Forcing you to burn the castle, we danced through the inferno, hoping the embers would keep our love alive.

As we walked out into the rubble our hands fell away leaving us to turn to ash.

~ mythology will be the death of us

A kiss on the forehead has never felt more deadly than the day you told me goodbye.

~ my third eye remains blind

Please do not put all your dreams into me.
For I do not think that my hands could hold your heart as delicately as you hold mine.

~ rough hands, soft heart.

You told me that you bought a devils ivy and that it changed you.

My breathing constricted my lungs.

You will never know the weight of the words that spilled, delicately from your mouth.

~ plants aren't forever

Two hearts longing to return to a home that doesn't exist anymore.

~ August

How could I possibly let you go, with this golden thread wrapping our memories around my heartstrings like that?

~ the strength of you

You told me we had to cut ties because it was too hard.

I agreed.

The burden of two halves not being whole, too great to bear.
But how can you sever the invisible thread that connects us,
no matter where we are?

~ the golden thread never breaks

It has always been the tale of two hearts trying to get back to a home that no longer exists.

I think this is where it ends.

~ our great young adult love story

Will my waves ever touch your shore again, or will I continue to crash into myself for the rest of my life?

I keep trying to find new places to go
Places that don't remind me of you.
Of us.

But it's hard, when for so long, you walked hand in hand in your little corner of the world together.

My god how I miss you.

I miss the way your fingers curled into my hair when we fell asleep.
I miss the way you say my name in the morning.
I miss the way you pull me close when we hear the rain outside.
I miss the smell of you, in summer by the ocean.
In winter, a cigarette on your lips.
I miss the space you take up in my bed it's never felt the same since you left.

It's the way you rub your hands over my skin, the looks you gave when you didn't think was I looking, how you held my wrist while you slept to make sure I was still there.

I miss everything that made you, us.

~ it's never going to go away.

You shuck my heart from my chest.

I am the oyster left with nothing but an empty home covered in salty water.

A new year is just another reminder that I'll be without you

~ *new year, same feelings.*

Your side of my bed isn't the same without you.

On cold nights
I miss lying under your covers,
electric blanket burning my ankles
your arm wrapped around my waist
hand resting on my chest
heartbeat in my ears

the chill of the night never comparing to rush your fingers gave me.

Arms wrapped around a sun warmed body.
A head nestled in your chest.
Hands clasped together as you sigh out long held breaths.
The smiles upon faces and the laughter lingering in the air.
A love that makes you feel alive.

Smaller shoes lay at the bottom of your bed, a different scent hangs on your jacket.
The smile that welcomes you in the morning looks like the one I used to give you.
Gazing eyes that adore the smile you have in your sleep, they are no longer mine.

~ you look like we used to.

I walk the halls in the dark, you were the light that led me home.

Your hands on my waist as you guide me into our room, the place where we kept secrets and our voices hushed.

Sounds only meant for us.

We lived there for five years, turbulent, beautiful, untouchable.

Then I blew the candles out.
I made everything go dark.
I made you suffer.
I made me ache.

Now,
your smile is wider and
your voice changes at the mention of her name.
My girlfriend
the words dripping from your lips like summers cold watermelon.

Two words to cut my heart and burn my soul, words that I used to hold close to my chest.

Now know how it feels,
to be on the receiving end of a dagger.
One ripped from its sheath and into flesh before you can see it.

I knew this day would come when I would be defenseless.
I had nothing, except
I'm so happy for you,
falling from my mouth like tears from my eyes
delicate, soft and quiet.

~ February isn't the month of love

You feel like summertime,
the warmth of you washes over my skin.

Your touch breeds goosebumps, my knees buckle at the thought of you.

I yearn for the summer
I'm the storm that signals the season is over.

The tears that cascade fill the rivers valleys you left behind.

Will the rains ever stop?

BLOOM

I hear your voice singing to me in my sleep, your hands holding my face under the light of the moon.

Delicate.

You cradle it porcelain, afraid to let go, keeping me together without hesitation.

Softness exudes from you, the spark that glides across my skin, your mouth and mine whispering together.

Then wake up knowing it will be hours until see you again, when my eyes are closed and my mind stops racing.

~ you showed up in a dream

I remember the night first saw you, there was a haze in the room and bass in my ears.
The sounds vibrating through my body, electricity melted from
my fingers.

Bodies moving slowly in front of me, your eyes finding mine as the crowd parted.

Nobody has ever looked at me that way again.

I knew it was you,

I think it's always going to be you.

I want him in the evening, bathed in the light of the moon,
tangled in the dark.

But it's your face want to see every morning,
the warm glow of summer kissing your face before I do.

Although I longed for him, I was waiting for you.
You taught me that waiting was worth it

~ patience is a virtue.

They used to ask me to write them stories about love.
I would tell them that I don't know if I would ever be able.
That my heart has been stolen, left to find its way back home,
out of sight in the dark.

In the heat of the summer you brought it back to me.
It's a lot easier to write stories about love once it returns.

Now when they ask me to tell them stories about love,
I smile and tell them about the day met you.

The way you call me *my darling* as if its the only name you've ever known
~ *love language pt I*

"You're my best friend, I mean it"
~ *love language pt II*

Nobody has ever looked at me the way you do
~ *love language pt III*

safety is the arms that you sleep in

~ girls don't need castles

Does my side of your bed miss me as much as my sheets miss you?
They scrunch themselves into a ball at the end of the bed, a reminder of where you used to be.

Is there still an imprint in your pillow from where my head would lay?

Does your skin still remember the lines I'd draw on it while you slept?

My hands miss finding their way towards yours in the dark. Fingers slotting together like jigsaw pieces.
The way they would find the knots in my back, melting into my skin like honey in the summer.

My feet are cold when you're not around, turning to ice slippers without you.

You're the fire that lit the embers in the bottom of my soles, you managed to warm me out of the loneliness that was left behind by the others.

~ I'm in trouble again

Today fell in love.

I fell in love with a girl at the coffee shop and how her hands wrapped around her pink ceramic cup.
Sharp, brightly coloured nails tapping against the sides, headphones drowning out external noise.

I fell in love with an older couple and the way they looked at each other.
It made me believe true romance exists.
They spoke quickly in Italian, eyes lighting up as they discussed family and the place they once called home.

I fell for a boy with a guitar in his hands who had his eyes closed on the tram.

I fell for a girl at the bar who video called her friend to show them how she rolled her first cigarette without help.

I fell in love with an older woman in a brightly coloured cardigan, her hair washed pink and her lipstick red.

Today, fell in love with life.

How sweet it is to feel so much for those who will never know.
You can fall in love every single day, if you look close enough.

The way you say my name under the light of a salt lamp is the sweetest song you've ever sung.

~ sing me to sleep tonight

I am the most important love I will ever know.
I am the strongest love I will ever feel.

~ you taught me this by saying goodbye

He was an endless vacation
salt water, citrus and cigarettes.
Sunshine never stolen by the clouds.

Months turned to years, sunset began to show,
inevitable.

Then you,
a gust out of nowhere,
the kind that drifts through winter pines.

Safe, stable, cosy a cabin fireplace.

The scent of summer stolen by pine and patchouli.

A storm passes through your body -
with the parting rain comes the sun
breaking through clouds.

There will always be an end to your unhappiness.

You must learn to weather the storm, guide your ship
through harsh winters.
When you arrive in spring, renewed, you will see that the
storm was worth it.

From rain comes life, through life we see miracles.

~ morning thoughts

How cruel the world was to make you feel undeserving.

That your light wasn't shining bright enough for anybody to see,
that you had to wait so long for opportunities.

The worlds intentions were not unkind
but the hands that dealt them were.

"Do you want anything?"

I just want you, as you are,
in this moment
the only distraction,
the lace of your dress.

I've been thinking about you a lot lately
the way you look when you step out of the shower,
an orange towel around your waist.

The way you walk and inch across the bed
cover me in fresh water kisses.
mint lingering on my cheeks.

~ March memories

We lay there silently willing the other to speak.

Your rapid heart,
the soundtrack to this scene in your bed.
A heightened pulse giving rhythm to the night.

My hands laced in yours, accompany the symphony.
Neither wants to be the first, trepidation on our lips.

Who will say *it?*

~ *I love you*

We fell asleep tangled in each other
My mind tangled up in someone else

Up in you
Up in who I'm becoming

The webs of my life interweave,
I try to make sense of them in the dark

As I try to figure out where this is leading
you roll over and whisper *I love you* in my ear and my
mind settles, breathing slows.

~ I don't know where this is going but like it

I've never laughed this much with anybody else.

~ *you have such a beautiful smile*

Your hand rests on my knee and your chin on my shoulder.
Is it possible to fall
into each other
even closer?

~ April is feeling really good

You left me a note that said was your greatest teacher,
helping you become who you are.

You were never my student.

You were my greatest gift,
letting me fall in love with who you were.

Seeing you bloom into yourself was one of lifes greatest adventures.

I'm endlessly proud of you.

~ never forget where you've been

www.ingramcontent.com/pod-product-compliance
Lightning Source LLC
Chambersburg PA
CBHW020330010526
44107CB00054B/2061